Dictionary for the Disenchanted

Dictionary for the Disenchanted

Bernard Rosenberg

HENRY REGNERY COMPANY • CHICAGO

Dedicated to Josephy Bensman who understands

Published by Henry Regnery Company
114 West Illinois Street, Chicago, Illinois 60610
Manufactured in the United States of America

Library of Congress Catalog Card Number: 72-80938

ILLEGITIMI NON CARBORUNDUM

Abolition of All Classes
A Utopian goal long cherished by Marxists who have lived to see it fulfilled in Academia.

Acupuncture
An ancient Oriental contribution to anesthesiology revived by Mao's politicized doctors purposely for the treatment of overeager anti-revisionists (red guards), infantile revisionists, paper tigers, and running dogs.

1

Ad-Man
A hard-headed but soft-spoken platitudinarian
trained to roll little butterballs off his tongue.

The Age of Trust
Traditionally, to all those under thirty, up to the thirtieth birthday. More liberally interpreted by those who have passed that milestone with a sigh of relief.

Airlines
Subsidized corporations that enjoy the rich man's welfare state more fully than most. They supply the speediest means of transporting affluent passengers from one desolation to another—with provision for such extras as cramped seating, ear-popping (induced not by air pressure but by a multi-media assault on the senses), and food-poisoning.

Al Fatah
A merry fellowship of romantic Middle Eastern pacifists, irresistibly attractive to American guerrillas (of either Jewish or Gentile persuasion) for their gaiety, camaraderie, pride of craft, and the stoicism with which they dispatch airline passengers, housewives, and farmers.

Alternative Culture
A bold, innovative, meaningful, spontaneous, and remunerative revolt against repressive middle-class standards that have long since vanished.

Apathy
A sense of awareness that alternates, in normal citizens, with mindless militancy. The two approaches to life are part of a dialectical sequence that ineluctably leads to a state of mental atrophy.

Apocalyptic Vision
A clear picture of impending doom best perceived by those who do their utmost to hasten its onset.

Arson
The last resort of a conscientious landlord for whom vandalism and intimidation have not afforded a proper return on his investment in choice property.

Artist
A man easily identified by his bizarre clothes, outrageous habits, long hair, insouciant manners, and other visible stigmata that render him indistinguishable from everyone else.

Autonomy
1. A will-o'-the-wisp in pursuit of which, men, women, and children exhaust themselves. 2. An illusion that encourages the belief that it is possible to attain control over others when self-control is impossible.

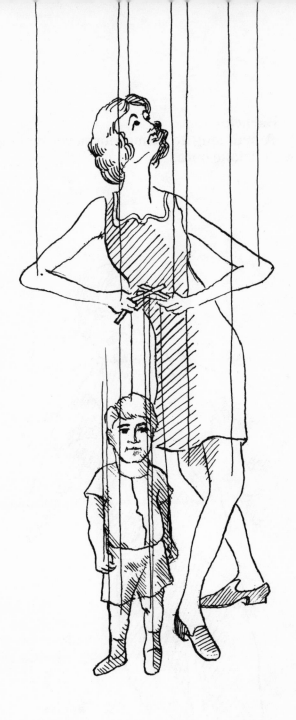

Bachelor
A man long acclaimed for never making the same mistake once.

Back to Nature
A rural extravaganza on a long macrobiotic death march with whole earth gurus leading their little charges through strip mines, rocky hollows, eroded lands, foul waters, and adjacent impedimenta.

Ball
To have promiscuous sexual intercourse presumably involving only the male genitalia.

Basic Desire
Above all, the desire that others should understand us—accompanied by the fear that they will.

Be-In
A gathering of juvenile tribes, and their elder associates, in which naked children roll joints while adults touch, feel, and make contact with oblivion, all in a state of blissful detumescence and without benefit of sensitivity training.

Benign Neglect
A judicious policy of official indifference to the black masses who, if decently housed and adequately educated, would cause acute unemployment in the professions dedicated to helping disadvantaged people.

Blacks
A non-chromatic reference to the strident minority of militants previously known as Negroes by those who respected people with dark skins and as blacks by those who did not.

Black Studies
A unique area of vocational training designed to instil pride in non-white students as a substitute for an education that would dangerously increase their employability.

Bomb
A relatively harmless instrument of persuasion that, if unheeded, provokes recourse to extreme methods.

Bomb Factory
A small non-union shop organized for the production of defective weapons by untrained workmen who, if injured, are unfairly deprived of state compensation. This type of factory is found in old-law tenements and opulent townhouses slated for accidental demolition.

Botulism

An exotic disease poor-mouthed by sour publicists who note that undiscriminating customers with a preference for certain kinds of Bon Vivant soup pay more to obtain the same mind-and body-blowing consequences they could get at a reasonable price from any old leaky, bumpy can of soup.

Bring the War Home

A battle cry derived from the earlier, somewhat more pacific, "Bring the Boys Home!" and fused with it to read, "Bring the boys home so that they can bring the war home." In other words, establish the Stateside Demilitarized Zone as a national epicenter of armed action and turn the United States into a continental free-fire zone where counterinsurgents can subdue native insurgents with the same dazzling success they have enjoyed abroad.

Capitalism

A socioeconomic system that, though no longer in existence, should nevertheless be abolished in favor of socialism. The distinction is important: capitalism is the exploitation of man by man, socialism the exact opposite.

Caricature

The essential ding-an-sich, the thing in itself without alteration, embellishment, or distortion.

CEPTIA

Committee to End Pay Toilets in America. A pressure group dedicated to the statutory prohibition of pay toilets whose spread its members view as a noisome infringement of human rights. Legislators who show sympathy for the movement are opposed by admirers of the terpsichorean art who point out that a beautiful native dance, the limbo, originated right here, and on no Caribbean shore, when an unknown choreographer slid under the door of a pay toilet—and that more such art may go down the drain if CEPTIA has its way.

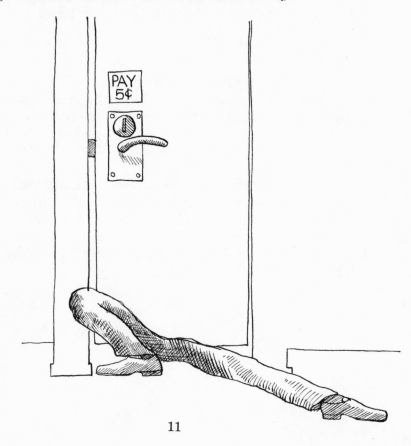

11

Change
Constancy; fixity; immutability.

Che Lives
There is no hero like a dead hero. By the same token, Ho lives; Malcolm lives. For many, Jesus lives. For a few, Adolph lives.

Chic
Fashionable in either radical or conservative terms, therefore "hip" or "in" and thus passé.

CIA
An organization of superspies peculiarly destined to be ignored when its intelligence reports are accurate and heeded when they are not.

Cigarettes
The little white slaves of yesteryear that are responsible for much cancer. A grim report by the United States Surgeon General prompted many Americans to foreswear nicotine and to consume larger quantities of food instead—causing obesity and death from heart failure.

Civility

An objectively counter-revolutionary attitude
that insidiously elicits good manners, good humor,
and peaceful intercourse; therefore, a powerful
fulcrum of the status quo; and, in the basic
existential or phenomenological sense, an assault on
everyone's dignity.

Coito Ergo Sum

A revised version of Descartes's dictum,
updated for groovy people who deeply dig the
pleasure principle.

College President

An awesome figure generally regarded as
unsatisfactory even before his installation,
occupying a hot seat he will soon be asked to vacate.
Yet, the president has options. Destined to preside
over the liquidation of academic freedom, the
president can handle his appointed task in any of
several ways. He can choose to be repressive or
benign, to call the cops or not to call them, to consult
or not to consult, to capitulate or to resist.

Columbus Day

A day of mourning for all of the indigenous and
most of the immigrant population of North, Central,
and South America.

Coming Out of the Closet
Bravely revealing about oneself what everybody always knew.

Community Control
Control of a community, preferably a school district or a slum neighborhood achieved by transferring power and boodle from a large number of outsiders to a small number of insiders.

Confrontation
A creative interaction that pits good revolutionary violence against bad counter-revolutionary violence.

Congressional Prerogatives
Constitutionally guaranteed rights and perquisites so jealously guarded by the world's greatest deliberative body that it refuses even to consider letting anyone else in on the deal.

Consciousness Expansion
Blowing one's mind in the interest of enlarging it.

Consciousness Raising
Brain washing.

Conservationists

Clausewitzian nature lovers who as sworn enemies of all official despoilers and polluters make war on the environment by other means.

Constructionist

Usually a *strict* constructionist. A legal expert who adheres faithfully and literally to the U.S. Constitution as that document was written in invisible ink. While paying lip service to the Old Confederacy, an S.C. is still a monarchist at heart. He knows that the Founding Fathers intended government to preserve the unity of state and church, control the press, throttle dissent, tap, bug, search, seize, disembowel Congress, and cretinize the courts.

16

Consumerism

The contemptible acquisition of *things*. The many who are revolted by consumerism as well as the capitalist manipulation and materialist philosophy that underlie it rebel by the massive purchase or theft (liberation) of such austere objects as fast cars, elaborate motorcycles, love beads, Indian bands, parkas, ponchos, handcrafted sandals, ornate boots, mod suits, skirts and unisex pants, leather jackets, jade necklaces, stereo sets, Apple records, guns, skis, snorkles, fancy wigs, tonsorial equipment, bongo drums, original Picassos, binoculars, eight-track tape recorders, strobe lights, German cameras, aphrodisiacs, Tarot cards, gourmet and/or health foods, and badly cut but not cut-rate narcotics.

Contraception

Criminal interference with the procreation of more living dolls.

Convict

A future recidivist confidently awaiting employment and full social acceptance in the hereafter.

Cooping

1. Curling up and going to sleep while on duty in a squad car. 2. A well-earned respite from being constantly and vigilantly on the take.

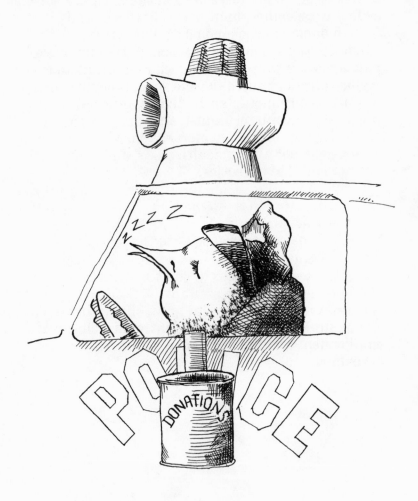

Co-optation
An odious attempt to seduce the proletariat by the distribution of higher education and good jobs for good pay to more poor people.

Correctional Facility
An institution such as those in Attica, New York, or San Quentin, California, in which wicked offenders are properly isolated, rehabilitated, caged, fed, tended, buggered, gassed, shot, and, above all, trained in the higher skills that will henceforth make them useful citizens.

Credibility Gap
The gnawing suspicion that once in a while the Administration may not be lying.

Criminal Classes
The lower classes; in contradistinction to the middle and upper classes in whose midst embezzlement, commercial and political bribery, fraud, force, misrepresentation, manipulation of stocks, fee-splitting, and price-fixing are not considered offenses.

Criminal Justice System
The speedy administration of legal codes that suffers neither from color blindness nor from insensitivity to socioeconomic status.

Crucifixion
A favored form of capital punishment in the ancient Levantine culture. More recently recommended by Martha Mitchell as suitable punishment for Senator Fulbright. If the idea catches on, hangmen will learn a new trade and convert Pennsylvania Avenue into the Via Dolorosa.

Curriculum
Under the new dispensation, unstructured classes in Raga-Rock, Zen Buddhism, Magic, Astrology, Karate, McLuhanism, and Drugs, punctuated at irregular intervals by choral recitation from the Little Red Book.

Custerism
1. The political process whereby an office holder eliminates his enemies before they eliminate him. 2. A suggested procedure for running amok that is scorned by finicky ideologues who believe they know better ways to commit suicide.

Day Care Center
A facility in which certain women who have borne children can unload them on other women—for a price about equal to the mothers' earning capacity. A day care center frees enlightened but fertile females from household drudgery. With it, and with no toddlers underfoot, they can overcome sexist prejudice whilst bracing themselves for the pleasures of factory work and office employment.

Death
The penultimate commercial transaction finalized by probate.

Decision Maker
A powerful telegenic do-gooder, perversely considered accountable for the errors of his superiors and subordinates.

Derangement
A generic term that covers all kinds of lunacy. Often expressed in oral, gustatory, and psychocaloric images. Accordingly, one goes "nuts" or "crackers" or "bananas," usually while in pursuit of "bread." This activity is wholly compatible with grinding down and gobbling up one's equally anthropophagous neighbors.

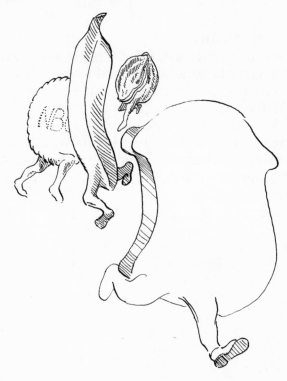

23

Desegregation
1. The mixture of children from lousy white schools with children from lousier black schools. 2. A policy supported by most Americans almost as vigorously as they oppose busing or any other means to attain the widely cherished national objective of equality of education.

Dialogue
A raucus monologue that, raised to the proper pitch, makes it impossible even for those who shout to hear that what they are demanding is non-negotiable.

Doing Your Own Thing
Insulating yourself from the perverted adult world by slavishly submitting to the tyranny of your peers.

Dollar
An exotic species, or specie, of currency that floats and flies in vertiginous downward curves.

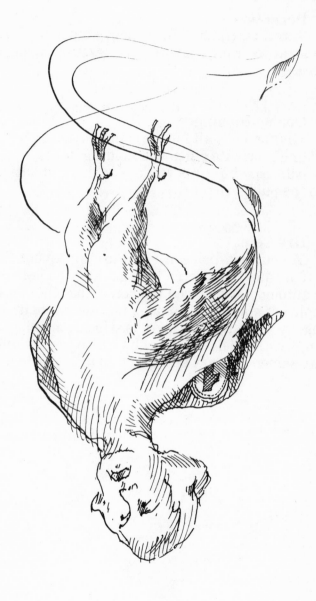

Dormitory
A residential hall for college students who come and go at their own risk with at least one armed escort.

Double Dipping
Giving one's all for the commonwealth by running a private office and holding down two political sinecures while reaching indefatigably into the public till.

Dry Cereal
A gourmet dish contrived to supplement the Staff of Life. Discovered by a genius who noticed, as the automobile replaced the horse, that there was a surplus of marketable oats. Kiddies and their progeny eat it up, but there is still too much. Happily, this delectation, which also carries untold nourishment, is now spreading to hitherto deprived peoples.

Ecology
The panacea that, if zero population growth fails, may yet be a final solution to the human problem. Its practitioners are so far on the right track that they have already greatly improved the environment by helping to eliminate several merely dangerous pollutants in favor of those that are probably carcinogenic and certainly lethal.

Econometrics
1. A quantitative scientific method of calculating and controlling employment, productivity, wages, and prices. 2. A subdiscipline of economics technically classified only a few notches below amateur meteorology.

Economic Development
A Third World religion, of which Maotheism is just the most popular variant.

EEOC
Equal Employment Opportunity Commission. A bipartisan federal agency devoted to achieving the same degree of alienation from work for every able-bodied American, regardless of race, creed, or sex.

Ego Tripping

Part of what Oscar Handlin has labeled the Counter-Copernican Revolution, which once again makes Man, or this time Me, Me, Me, the center of the universe.

Entrapment
A clever tactic used by many policemen to apprehend criminals—unless the criminals happen to be policemen, in which case this illegal operation is a throwback to the otherwise admirable practices of Joe McCarthy.

Entropologist
A student of Man, formerly an anthropologist. Claude Lévi-Strauss introduced the modification when it occurred to him that his unit of study was rapidly running down and out.

Establishment
The powers-that-be.

Anti-Establishment
The powers-that-may-be.

Ethnic Group
A collective identity invented in America for diverse individuals united by little save their lack of common origins.

Evacuation
Withdrawal from a building that is, or is rumored to be, filled with explosives placed therein by revolutionaries who might otherwise be preparing to occupy it.

Existentialism
A fashionable school of philosophy, groovy enough for swingers to dig, especially when set forth with the elegance of Professor Paul Ricoeur, who asks: "Where else but in the tension between the positing of the in-itself-identical and the transauthentic simultaneity of its negativing at the heart of the existential word is it that the deep tragicity manifests itself within the subjectivity of the non-understanding of the incomprehensible?"

Expediency
1. Political practicality; good sense; realism. 2. The force that propels a candidate to the solid center just as it crumbles, evaporates, and disappears.

Family Counseling
A catalyst that causes isolated nuclei that commonly float around each other at a distance to collide and explode.

Fat Cats
Welfare recipients living high on the hog while respectable folks are deprived of messengers, shoeshine boys, maids, gardeners, elevator operators, parking attendants, and latrine cleaners.

Femininity
Warmth, gentleness, sensitivity, and compassion embodied in such otherwise heterogeneous women as Oveta Culp Hobby, Bernardine Dohrn, Louise Day Hicks, Margaret Mitchell, and Valerie Solanis, who deceive no one when they hide behind a masculine facade of brutality.

Fink
A person of some other persuasion.

Fiscal Responsibility
1. Penny-pinching that produces a calculated equilibrium between income and outlay. 2. That which is chronically subverted by Democratic spendthrifts but sacred to Republican Presidents dedicated to full-employment deficit budgeting.

Flower Children
Ex-Kamikazes or Kamikazes-in-the-making.

Foreign Aid
Popularly defined as taxing poor people in rich countries for the benefit of rich people in poor countries.

Foreign Policy
The systematic cultivation of enemies and the alienation of friends until they too become enemies.

Frankfurter

A pure all-beef product composed of fat, water, various interesting additives like sodium nitrate and sodium nitrite, plus such edible offal as esophagi, lips, snouts, ears, hair, and muscle tissue taken from carcasses of "4D" (dead, dying, diseased, and disabled) cattle, all palatably spiced with insect fragments and rodent remains.

Fraternity
A social and political ideal that we gladly accept as long as it remains clear which one of us is Big Brother.

Free All Political Prisoners
All prisoners *are* political. Therefore, free them or else how will there be room for the rest of us?

Free Enterprise
A huge area of the American economy still noticeable to observers with peripheral vision after they subtract the public sector, conglomerates, federally supported agriculture, monopolies, duopolies, and oligopolies.

Free Speech
1. A bourgeois affectation. 2. Interference with law 'n' order. 3. Further proof of how correct the French are when they assert that *les extrèmes se touchent.*

Front runner
A candidate in the enviable position of being so far ahead that he is sure to lose. (See *Peaking*)

35

Futurologists
Twentieth-century astrologers handicapped by
tunnel vision who, unable to apprehend the present,
helpfully extrapolate it.

Game Plan
An elaborate, inflexible but modifiable or
reversible scheme for political election to the
presidency.

Gay Liberation
Odd man in and on top of everybody.

Generation Gap
A chasm, amorphously situated in time and
space, that separates those who have grown up
absurd from those who will, with luck, grow up
absurd.

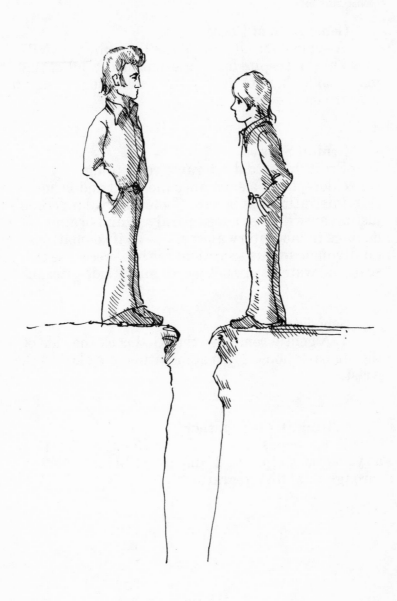

Generation of Peace
A symbol for citizens of the Republic who will soon enjoy a respite from international conflict that may enable them to lick their wounds long enough to prepare for the next war.

Genital Sprays
Fruit-flavored deodorants containing hexachlorophine, a substance the Food and Drug Administration has labeled "potentially dangerous" just because "tests caused paralysis and brain damage in laboratory animals"—as if combatting mildly malodorous secretions without recourse to soap and water were not worth minor side-effects.

Genocide
1. A gentle reminder that God *is* on the side of the big battalions. 2. An admonition or a slap on the wrist.

Getting It All Together
1. The opposite of sorting it all out; collectively, a synthesis of ciphers. 2. Imperceptible integration through total disintegration.

GNP

Gross National Product. Also, Gross National Pollution. Together, they synthesize into exceedingly Gross National Progress.

God Is Dead

Nietzsche's chestnut reheated in the crucible of Crisis Theology. In some quarters a source of despair, and yet not everywhere, as we learn from a topical graffito that goes: "God is dead, but don't worry. Mary's pregnant again."

Going Ape

1. Swinging, but without trees. 2. A manic-depressive seizure that symbolizes the animated biped's true simian nature.

The Great Cultural Revolution
1. A recent outburst of gorgeous preadolescent Chinese Communist exuberance. 2. Youthful spontaneity controlled and directed by the state (for a whole year, with tender guidance from above, every child washed his own brain and that of any adult within reach). 3. The nonviolent eruption that shook a billion Asians, but left them only momentarily dismembered.

Green Power
The bread—or dough to dodderers who leavened it—that brings not happiness but affliction, widely exchanged, by the descendants of those who unscrupulously made money, for flower power or fire power.

Growing Up Absurd
Paul Goodman's locution for the difficulties experienced by an earlier generation of adolescents who are now the parents of children growing up hallucinogenic *and* absurd.

Halfway House
A way station to nowhere. (See *Nowhere*)

Halloween
A happy holiday that brings out the best in frolicsome adults who, when asked for a treat, give small children malted milk balls, tootsie rolls, and fresh apples filled with mescaline, LSD, crushed glass, sharp pins, and razor blades.

Handyman
1. An expert and expensive clod—a technician, an electrician, a plumber. 2. A man who can never be paid too much for keeping our gadgets in disrepair and freeing us from our unnatural dependence on technology.

Hard-Core Mediocrity
The average politician; typically, Richard Milhous Nixon, his family, his entourage, his supporters, and his admirers.

Head Start
1. Preparation for the penal colony. 2. A program designed in bureaucratic miasmas for disadvantaged children who have had little opportunity to learn all they will need to know about pupil-processing.

Hipster
1. Anyone who passes the acid test by dropping diathilamide, preferably while moving from Haight to hate. 2. Someone who adopts customs that go in one era and out the other.

History
A nearly defunct field of study that is of value only to the extent that it glorifies everything previously debased, and vice versa.

Honesty
The most important thing in life. Unless you really know how to fake *it*, you'll never make it.

Househusband

A man who, though ravaged by vulva envy and weary from his daily round of shopping, cleaning, cardplaying, televiewing, taxiing the big children, and nursing the baby, is still expected to look attractive when his spouse returns from her hard day at the office.

Housing Shortage
A metaphysical condition characterized decades ago by Henry Morgan as an ugly rumor circulated by people who have no place to live.

Hypocrisy
A personal trait, a *sine qua non* for political and commercial success, yet curiously ascribed *only* to other, usually older, people.

Inner Space
A void whose chemically induced exploration may take the psyched-out, the freaked-out, the stretched-out, and the flaked-out more than one lifetime to circumnavigate.

Innovation
A novel device of any sort by which administrators recently installed in power learn why their way of doing things also does not work.

Integration
The latest indignity concocted by Machiavellian liberals, tirelessly pursuing their sinister campaign to create racial harmony. Fortunately for national stability, this plot has, thus far, been thwarted by the combined and heroic efforts of such brothers under the skin as Black Nationalists, White Citizens Councils, and Southern Klansmen awaiting appointment to the Supreme Court.

Intellectuals
Effete pawns aspiring to be heroic knights; they do little but talk of overthrowing the military-industrial-academic complex to which all of them are happily enslaved.

Ivory Tower
1. A haven for the contemplative scholar who can descend its spiral staircase from the First Circle to the Lower Depths. 2. An ivied retreat for those bent on committing menticide.

46

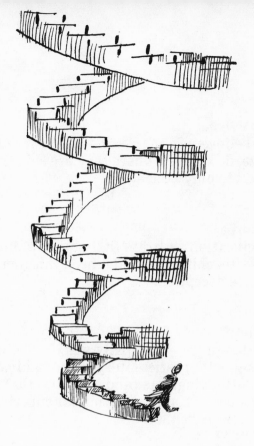

Jesus Freaks
True believers in the Second or Third Coming who realize, down deep where they are superficial, that God is the only atheist.

Job Corps
A pacification program that helped radicalize dropouts by teaching them advanced chicanery and postgraduate deception.

Kinesics
Body language, principally winking, blinking, and nodding, with gesticulatory accompaniments. Viewed by ethnolinguists (and animals other than man) as a mode of communication far superior to the written or spoken word.

Let It All Hang Out
An injunction to conceal everything but one's private parts.

Life

A terminal disease afflicting all living creatures, of which such periods as adolescence and aging are merely symptoms.

Life Cycle

A biosocial sequence that omits only one stage—maternity—as it proceeds from infancy through childhood to adolescence and decrepitude.

Like

In current usage, an all-purpose expletive. Along with "you know," "hopefully," "dig," "cool," and "man," it has so enriched American English that we can henceforth do without most of the remaining 600,000 words that still clutter last year's unabridged and out-of-date dictionaries.

Long-term Care Facility

Known in the unprofessional past as a nursing home. Then and now, and by any name, a splendid establishment in which the aged and indigent are nourished on all the compassion society can spare.

Loot-In
A revolutionary strategem conceived in some circles on the Left as a massive blow at department stores, and thereby "at the property fetish that underlies genocidal war."

Low Profile
A shadow image of near-nothingness so skillfully projected through the media that one scarcely notices the absence of a head.

Lunatic Lib
An organization that, according to Walter Goodman, represents the Veterans of State Hospitals, a pressure group lobbying against strait jackets and for community control of sanity tests, which, at present, are unfairly skewed in favor of sane people.

Lust
An emotion that the poet Swinburne rightly admonished us never to degrade by confusing with love.

Lycanthropy
1. A wholesome wolfish disposition that causes men to tear one another apart. 2. A sprightly manifestation of man's animal nature that is currently enjoying a sweet and healthy recrudescence.

Mafia
A fictitious term slanderously applied to gentlemen of the underworld, often of Sicilian extraction, who really belong in the upperworld. This group is also not known as the Cosa Nostra or the Syndicate and differs not at all in disposition and only slightly in activities from those groups whose reputations remain unbesmirched and whose job is to put it out of business—the F.B.I., police, legislators, the Mob.

Mainliner
1. Formerly, a Philadelphia gentleman. 2. Now, anyone's son or daughter.

Make Love, Not War
1. Be surly to everybody. 2. Fight only your enemies—nearly everybody—to the death.

Man
A biodegradable but nonrecyclable animal blessed with opposable thumbs capable of grasping at straws.

Medical Doctor
A professional man who cannot heal himself except with greenbacks.

Melting Pot
A cultural receptacle for forging steel by striking wet matches in a vain attempt to ignite incombustible matter.

Menstruate
A flagrant example of sexism built into the language. When corrected, it will read *womenstruate*.

Metropolis
1. Necropolis. 2. A concentrated collection of fetid villages, nurtured on graft, crime, and smog, bathed in politics, and held together by the strangest human bond: the determination to take and not to be taken in a constant war of all against all.

Millionaires

An underprivileged minority composed of men who, although they strenuously clip coupons, look carefully after their investments and oil wells, buy and sell municipal bonds, tend their cattle, and scrupulously spray their orange groves, are rewarded by an ungrateful government with nothing more than total tax exemption.

Minutemen

Welcome proof of continuity in the national history, these are men on-the-ready to make or break any American Revolution.

Mother

The first half-word most Americans learn.

Mystic Drug Experience

Popping, dropping, snorting, and smoking one's way through Nirvana to Cloud Cuckooland.

National Defense

1. A high priority item through whose expansion we keep the peace. 2. A prudent allocation of American treasure to protect people from war by involving them in an unlimited arms race. Similarly, dypsomaniacs stock up on whisky to become teetotalers.

National Liberation

1. An exchange of local tyrants for foreign masters. 2. The first step to sanguinary civil war. 3. Balkanization, or a redrawing of frontiers so that the Third World can be retribalized and *then* pulverized.

Necrophilia

1. The perfectly natural but widely condemned wish for sexual relations with a corpse. Enlightened people believe that the practice should be permitted between consenting adults. 2. A passion for justice.

NEP
New Economic Policy, twice adopted in the twentieth century, first by V. I. Lenin, to restore a measure of capitalism in Soviet Russia and, much later, by Richard Nixon, to abolish the remnants of capitalism in North America.

The New Ethic
Kant upside down. Hence the directive: always treat man as a *means*, never as an *end*. This handy ethic is especially to be found among office holders.

The New Morality
A state of de-regulation that begins with simple anomie or normlessness and by and by matures into a higher delirium called atonie or listlessness approximating lifelessness.

Nice Guys Never Win
1. A half truth, the other half being that nasty guys never win either. 2. Nobody ever wins; man is a born loser.

Night School
An educational institution in which grownups who apply themselves can learn why they are as unteachable as their children in day school.

Nihilism

A brilliant political recipe that enables man to break eggs and heads without making omelettes or revolutions.

Nixonomics

A dazzling bundle of indefensible doctrines derived from Adam Smith, Karl Marx, and John Maynard Keynes, used in whatever order or mixture is best calculated to preserve the status quo.

Nixspeak

First cousin to Newspeak. Especially well illustrated in a few examples assembled by the writer, TRB: "I have pledged to the American people that I would submit a balanced budget for 1971." (Budget Message, February, 1971) "The most significant agreement in the history of the world." (On devaluation of the dollar) "Of the many receptions that have been held in this room, this is one of the most exciting of all." (Comment on an all-star baseball reception at the White House) "I will not take this nation down the road of wages and price control however politically expedient that may seem." (Repeatedly, in one succinct version or another) "I would not agree to admitting Red China to the United Nations." (October, 1968) "This certainly has to be the most historic telephone call ever made from the White House. . . . This is the greatest week in the history of the world since Creation." (Telephone conversation with the first astronaut to land on the moon)

No Accident
As in, "It was no accident that the President finally imposed wage and price (and not profit) controls." An act attributed to their colleagues by those responsible for rational planning and considerations of public welfare that the same group previously had strenuously opposed.

Nostalgia
A word derived from the Greek, *nostros,* meaning a return home, and *algos,* meaning a pain. People nowadays tend to remember the first part and forget the second, but even they have recently noticed that nostalgia isn't what it used to be.

Nothing
What man should always expect, even though it is considerably more than most men will ever get.

Not Really
The handiest answer to such personal questions as: "Are you a pacifist?" "Do you believe in God?" "In socialism?" "Do you like your mother and father?" "School?" "Tripping?" "*Anything?*"

Now
1. A little while ago. 2. Day before yesterday. 3. Last year.

Nowhere

There, as in Gertrude Stein's comment about Oakland, California, "There is no there there."

Nuclear Family

A volatile, fissionable, barely controllable, and potentially explosive social unit composed of parents and children. This monstrosity cannot be used for peaceful purposes and should be banned forthwith.

Nuclear Sufficiency

A state of unpreparedness incapable of producing anything more than minor holocausts. It must yield to Nuclear Supremacy, a pre-condition that is absolutely essential for our total annihilation.

Off

A preposition struggling successfully to become a verb, e.g., "Off the President," "Off the pigs," "Off everybody." Roughly equivalent to "Smash," or "Liquidate," or - more delicately, "Murder!"

O.I.

Orgasmic impairment. A sexual disability on the distaff side as analyzed by David Reuben, M.D., who, never having studied Clit. Lit. at first hand, has no serviceable remedy to offer.

Oldsters

1. An antedeluvian subspecies of impoverished supernumeraries. 2. A golden-aged but gruesome Fifth Estate. 3. The *nouveaux pauvres*.

Operation Intercept
Billed as a program to diminish the exportation of hemp, but actually an adjunct of the President's New Economic Policy designed to give the economy in inflationary shot in the arm by turning users onto costlier drugs.

Overkill
The perpetually inadequate capacity to slaughter every creature on earth five hundred times over—and then to do it again for good measure.

Paraprofessionals
Uncredentialed incompetents who assist certified incompetents in various educational, medical, and occupational programs that alleviate no one's distress except, occasionally, their own.

Parents
Adults who should be seen but not heard.

Participatory Democracy
Decision making for everyone by a few self-appointed leaders of a small segment of the young middle-class white elite.

Peace
A relatively tranquil period in international relations over which Republican Presidents preside during prolonged depressions that Democratic Presidents terminate by going back to war.

Peaking
1. Surfacing months before a national party convention, which is to say, prematurely; suffering exposure, that is, overexposure. 2. Allowing the electorate an early glimpse into the candidate and thereby inviting his certain defeat.

Pentagonese
The special language whose invocation obliterates ballistic missiles and nuclear warheads by relabeling them launchers and force loadings.

Permissiveness
The parental approach that fosters free and unrestricted growth in youngsters who become campus rebels. By contrast, as several studies show, firmness and discipline in an authoritarian family atmosphere fashion model youngsters who become campus rebels.

Pessimist
Same as optimist, but better informed.

Petishism

A wholly rational fixation, on, and preference for, any nonhuman domesticated animal.

Pigs

(See also *Policemen*)

Used interchangeably and increasingly in pop literature with the less self-explanatory *Geeks*. In either form, an important addition to the contemporary lexicon. "Fuzz" will do, too, but exclusively in its pristine reference to policemen. "Pigs" has been broadened to encompass most citizens of the United States.

Ping-Pong

1. Asian diplomacy, a variation of Yin-Yang, Hong Kong, tick-tock, zig-zag, and Chinese checkers. 2. A spectator sport requiring violent oscillations of the head.

Policemen

(See also *Pigs*)

1. Proud professionals who belong to trade unions because they are exploited workers.
2. Champions of law and order with an interest less in the Constitution they are sworn to serve than in the profits to be made from protecting the public.
3. Upright civil servants engaged in obtaining a share of the wealth of vice lords and reducing the excess profits of small-scale entrepreneurs.

Political Problems
A category divisible into: (1) those problems that solve themselves; (2) those for which there is no solution.

Politician
A public figure of unquestionable integrity and a sharp eye for the buck whose association with the Mafia is either known or unknown.

Pop Porn
A reductio ad obscenum involving twosomes, threesomes, foursomes, and "moresomes" bent on making the world safe for pornography.

Poverty
A condition certain privileged youth find so enviable that they have enthusiastically embraced it. Some take up residence in roach-and-rat-infested tenements, pick garbage pails and panhandle; a few persist in this pattern even after remittance checks from indulgent parents have stopped. This abstract condition requires only the widespread distribution of bootstraps to disappear from the vocabulary even of aspiring politicians.

Power
An impalpable substance that grows out of the barrel of a gun and recoils on its user.

Pragmatism

A distinctively American philosophy whose only failing is that it does not work.

Preventive Reaction

(See also *Pentagonese*)

An action antecedent to an event that does not take place, *viz.*, bombing North Vietnam in retaliation for attacks the enemy somehow fails to make.

Professor

1. A small businessman using the letterhead of a large university. 2. An informer who denounces revolutionary students for following his instructions. 3. A paralytic immobilized by the absence of clear-cut directives. 4. A reactionary, prepared to clobber student nihilists unless they come to power—who in that case will support their every wish and whim. 5. A liberal, rational man, on his way to bleeding ulcers, neural disorders, coronaries, another profession, early retirement, or premature death.

Progress

Steady advancement particularly in the technological sphere. A case in point is the progression from the handicraft production of death, with, for example, a machete, to the mass production of death, with, for example, a flamethrower, a multiple independently targeted reentry vehicle, or—the latest advance—the anti-personnel-plastic-pellet bomb.

The Protestant Ethic

An austere Calvinist creed of work and thrift to which Chinese Communists and European Stalinists, as well as many American Catholics and Jews, but very few WASPS, fervently adhere.

Psychosis

Severe mental disorder. Called insanity in legal language, psychosis has never been a problem in the western world, where it has been effectively contained either by chaining, burning, mutilating, and otherwise exorcising diabolical spirits, or, later on, by confinement with solicitous custodial care, culminating in beneficent shock treatment and emotional decapitation through lobotomies, lobectomies, and topectomies. These excellent cures have now been superseded by powerful drugs that transform patients into ambulatory vegetables.

Public Housing
A residential and financial cornucopia emitting largesse for developers, builders, lenders, and wreckers, all to help Uncle Sam become a super-slumlord and make the poor noticeably poorer.

Quiet Desperation
The existential experience common to the bulk of men in Thoreau's time; with the increase in the decibel level today, this experience has become one of *noisy* desperation.

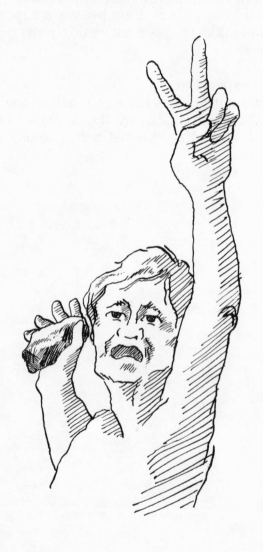

70

Radical
A person whose left hand does not know what his other left hand is doing.

Reclamation
A difficult job assigned to pilots who have warmed up for the bigger challenge that lies ahead by dropping high explosive, defoliant, and napalm on Vietnam, Cambodia, Laos. . .

Redistricting
A democratic maneuver by which carefully selected legislators are gerrymandered out of politics so that their successors can enjoy their proper feed at the trough.

72

Reform Politics
The democratization of graft, based on a sound premise: that men of integrity have been denied their fair share for long enough.

Relevance
In the academic context, a demand to establish new, pragmatically oriented types of higher education that prepare students for the real world—involving total abandonment of the present pragmatically oriented types of higher education that prepare students for the real world.

Relive It
What all of those who do not read history are condemned to do. In this, they resemble all of those who do read history.

Remediation
A sisyphean task at which academics labor so assiduously that many Colleges of Liberal Arts are nowadays accurately designated Colleges of Remedial Arts. Robert Maynard Hutchins looms large as a prophet who anticipated that the Three R's, Reading, Riting and Rithmetic, would be replaced by the Six R's, Remedial Reading, Remedial Riting and Remedial Rithmitic. Not even he, however, foresaw that these specialties would reach up and envelop candidates for the Ph.D. degree.

Repression

The highly desirable outcome of all conflict between established authority and rebels young and old, according to the theory of which revolutionary electoral preferences point to such candidates as Ronald Reagan and George Wallace. The extreme usefulness of this theory was first illustrated in Weimar when the German Communist party assured its own glorious future by contributing to the success of Adolph Hitler.

Revisionism

An opportunistic commitment to *limited* terror tactics.

Rotten Apple

The fruit by which an entire barrel should not be judged. Hence if there are 3,200 men in the municipal constabulary of whom two are honest, a good citizen judges all of them not by the 3,198 crooks but by the two saints—who, before they are formally discharged, will be suspended and tried for informing on their fellows.

74

Sacrés du Printemps

Springtime rituals that include disruptions, occupations, busts, and closures. These ceremonials occur at that climactic moment when the social crisis reaches its height: just before final exams.

Scholarship

An anachronistic and by no means harmless pastime suitable to dotards and other survivors of an age suffused with those false values of "learning" and "cultivation of the mind."

The Sexual Revolution
Conquest of the last frontier, involving the efficient management and manipulation of reproductive organs for the purpose of establishing the New Puritanism.

Shoplifting
Inventory shrinkage whose useful purpose is to reduce monetary deflation in the soft goods department.

Shredding
A mechanical process long used for the refinement of wheat lately transferred by ITT to corporate documents with signal success.

The Silent Majority
A Homeric reference to the dead. This concept has been revived through alliterative incantation by Spiro Agnew, a Greek philosopher of the Eleatic School whose voice resounds through all the ectoplasmic catacombs of Middle America.

Skinner Box
A cage with many amenities devised to ease the process of conditioning infinitely manipulable children so that they too can reach the level of captive rats, monkeys, pigeons, and chickens.

Social Worker
A not-so-well trained sadistic detective directly descended from Lady Bountiful.

Society
A throng of insects swarming around and below the surface of civilization.

Speed Ball
Mixture of heroin and cocaine snorted through the nostrils, administered hypodermically, or inserted into the anus. A good dose induces simultaneous depression and elation, only occasionally resulting in death.

Standards
High criteria established by authorities as a rule for the measure of quality; best exemplified in the meat industry where products graded U.S. Good, Choice, and Prime are translated by the knowledgeable consumer as Fat, Fatter, and Fattest.

Stars and Stripes
A representation of national unity, whether fluttering in the breeze, worn, torn, burned, or, most appropriately, washed.

Stinging
Accepting payment for goods or services and then failing to deliver them: "Taking the money without turning the trick." A practice that could give politics, if not prostitution, a bad name.

Straight
1. Sober; rational. 2. Heterosexual. 3. Tolerant, dull.

Street Culture
Urban idyll enacted in the metropolis where people periodically shoot up for a high the better to enjoy their pastoral surroundings.

Strontium 90
A substance that poisoned an earlier, preorganic generation as yet unaware of the toxic delights of asbestos, talc, or tuna and swordfish saturated in mercury.

Suburbia
Swinging parts of inner city life transplanted to the grasslands by migrants to facilitate their escape from what they bring with them.

Suicide
Self-destruction or, more precisely, "murder in the 180th degree," a competitive sport in which the United States does not yet rank Number One. But it tries harder.

Sunshine Patriot
One who abstains from violent demonstrations on rainy days.

Tell It Like It Is
Obfuscate by doing violence to the language.

Theory
Bullshit.

Threads
Outer garments of those who are able to get it all together sartorially, permitting them to remain loose and cool—provided they suffer no serious rip-offs.

TLS

The *Times Literary Supplement* of London. A beacon piercing through the murky air created by other more popular journals that have brought English prose to its present low estate, as this passage from a recent issue amply demonstrates: "If it should happen that the arbitrary character of the delimitation imposed by school taxonomies, between what deserves to be taught (the "classics") and what does not, be unmasked—when, for instance, the inertia of the educational system, with its tendency to retain on the syllabus anything that has ever found its way there, goes too directly against the interests of this or that category of privileged users—the principles underlying these hierarchies and, a fortiori, the *petitio principii* implied in the very fact of hierarchization are neither perceived nor challenged because, following arbitrary indoctrination whose tendency is to conceal the arbitrary character of that indoctrination and of what it has taught, the differences produced by the application of this arbitrary hierarchization principle are experienced as being part of the very nature of the objects which they differentiate, as it were logically pre-existing the principle of which they are products." So it goes.

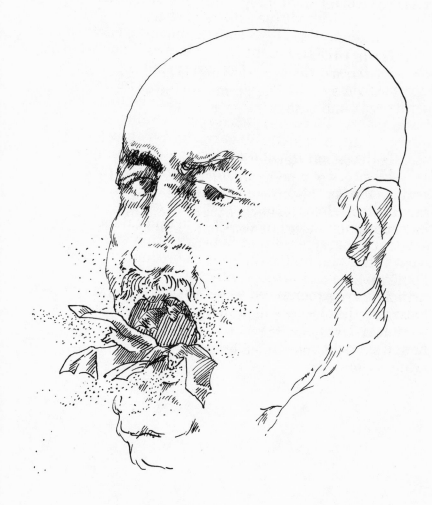

81

Totalitarianism

A dirty word gratuitously applied to the New Left by critics whose insensitivity precludes them from apprehending the well-known but subtle distinction between totalitarianism of the Right and totalitarianism of the Left.

Trade Unions

Lower middle-class repositories of false consciousness, reflecting an insane preoccupation with bread and butter.

Transsexual Revolutionaries

Members of a political cult that derives its rationale from this prolegomenon to a new manifesto: "Homosexuals of the world, unite! You have nothing to lose but your balls and chains."

Trashing

An earnest effort to improve the ecological balance of the environment by the smashing of windows, desks, doors, typewriters, bookstores, and flower shops, accompanied by the setting of one, two, or more small fires.

Troops
Armed and uniformed Americans formally organized in a complex hierarchy and informally reorganized into: (1) juicers, always on the sauce; (2) heads, devoted to hash or speed; and (3) freaks, who re-enlist to stay on cheap skag.

Twentieth Century
1. Modern times. 2. A period in which mankind waited first for Lefty and then for Godot—finally relinquishing any hope that either would ever arrive.

Ulster
A territorial plum with vast resources contentedly shared by Protestants and Catholics until the Ecumenical movement reactivated it as a proving ground for *Pacem in Terris*.

Underachiever
A little lad who has yet to progress from glue sniffing to hard drugs.

Uniform Crime Reports
Dual crime reports. Figures and graphs distributed as a public service by the FBI, scientifically computed to indicate: (1) a sharp increase in the crime rate, necessitating larger appropriations of money with which to combat it; and (2) a significant decline in the crime rate, reflecting the ever greater efficiency of law enforcement.

Unisex
Fashionable attire used interchangeably by men and women. A source of consternation to transvestites.

University
1. A medieval institution first established in Bologna, Oxford, and Paris, that, although scandalously outliving its time, has proved to be adaptable. 2. Most accurately defined for the present by an editor of *American Scholar* as a therapeutic center, an adventure playground, and a partial solution to the problem of unemployment.

Up Front
Openly, freely, frankly, and sincerely duplicitous.

Up Tight
Pertains to a state of anxiety that afflicts all inhabitants of Squaresville (sometimes known as Cancer Gulch). From that center of infection it has spread to everyone else including hippies, yippies, crazies, mad dogs, cool cats, junkies, and heads.

USA
Erroneously decoded by the late e.e. cummings as The Benighted States of Hysterica (E Pluribus Eunuch); actually, the United States of America, one of the few surviving republics where, if you do not first get killed, you can still make a killing.

The Vanishing Adolescent
A prolific breed. More visible and less imperturbable than the Vanishing Indian.

VAT
Value added tax. A progressive levy on all the people, similar to most taxes weighted against those least able to pay, and designed to complement the regressive income tax that only hits some of them.

Vegetarian Party
The one really radical party in American Politics: it alone goes to the roots of matters.

War

Recourse to arms for the settlement of international disputes. Reprehensible in south Asia when initiated by the world's most populous democracy, but admirable in southeast Asia when perpetrated by the world's oldest democracy.

War Room

A military enclosure far removed from the battlefield where faulty intelligence, defective data, and other revelations are programmed into computers that seldom go wrong.

Washington, D. C.
A sleepy southern town where the walls have ears and the ears have walls.

Waste
An active verb. The imperative form is favored by some military officers in the Far Eastern theater of war, as in "Waste 'em," a command to massacre aged Indochinese men and unarmed women along with their babies. Widely known as "No big deal."

Weathermen
Young political merteorologists who carefully observe which way the wind is blowing them—to prison or to Kingdom Come.

Where It's At

A grammatical and syntactical improvement upon the obsolete form, *Where It Is*. *Where It's At* parallels *Where the Action Is*—not yet successfully prepositionalized—and means roughly: where the firebombs go off, where the Molotov cocktails explode, where the dynamite is detonated.

Winding Down

1. Actually, winding *up*. 2. Expanding, enlarging, extending, and otherwise cleverly ending an interminable war.

Wisdom
The recognition that things are worse than they were but better than they are going to be.

Women's Liberation
A many splintered thing. A movement to restore to women all the rights they never had. The tendency is still diffuse, but two subgroups are discernible: the moderates who merely propose to castrate all men, and the extremists who propose to slay them. If Stokely Carmichael's widely quoted dictum ("The position of women in our movement should be prone") is accurate, women—apart from those nymphomaniacs who know a good thing when they see one—do indeed have reason to be aggrieved.

Work
"The only dirty four-letter word in the English language," according to the eminent lexicographer Abbie Hoffman.

Youthquake
An eruption followed by a twitch, a tic, and much sullen or ashen silence.

Zonked
1. Stoned. 2. Temporarily quiescent.
3. Unnaturally silent. 4. A state preliminary to loud protest and violent street action.